Contents

On the road   6

Types of traffic   8

Walk or cycle?   10

Busy or quiet?   12

People who help   14

Traffic controls   16

Stop, look and listen   18

Parking problems   20

Making an area safer   22

Old and new   24

Traffic around the world   26

Useful words   28

Some answers   29

Index   30

About this book   30

On the road

We travel on roads to get to other places.

Some roads are very wide.

Some roads are narrow.

Traffic is any vehicle with wheels that drives on a road.

These children are going to school in a car.

What sort of traffic do you see on your way to school?

Types of traffic

Some types of traffic carry things people need. This lorry is taking food to a supermarket.

Some traffic carries lots of passengers. People get on and off this bus at bus stops.

Some types of traffic are only used in an emergency. Sirens and flashing lights warn other traffic that they go fast!

Fire engines take firefighters to put out fires.

Ambulances carry sick or injured people to hospital.

Who else uses the road? Turn the page to find out.

Walk or cycle?

Pedestrians are people who walk next to roads. They walk on the pavement.

Children should hold an adult's hand to keep safe when crossing the road.

There are cycle lanes for people
who ride bikes on roads.

Cyclists
should wear
bright,
reflective
clothes so
that drivers
can see them.

What else should you do to be safe on your bike?

Busy or quiet?

This road is quiet.

There are mostly houses and very little traffic.
There are no offices or other places of work.

This road is busy with traffic.

Many people come here to visit the shops and to work in the offices.

Who helps keep us safe on busy roads?
Turn the page to find out.

People who help

Many people work to keep us safe on the road.

Road Safety Officers teach children about road safety.

Lollipop people stop vehicles so children can cross.

Traffic police keep drivers and pedestrians safe. They wear a bright yellow jacket so that they can be seen easily.

If a car breaks down, a truck comes to tow it off the road.

How do traffic controls help? Turn the page to find out.

Traffic controls

Traffic controls tell vehicles how fast they can go - and when to stop!

This speed sign tells drivers not to go faster than 30 miles per hour.

This red traffic light tells vehicles to stop so that people can cross.

What traffic controls are there near your school?

Nina's class marks the traffic controls in their local area on a street plan. They use a code for the different traffic controls.

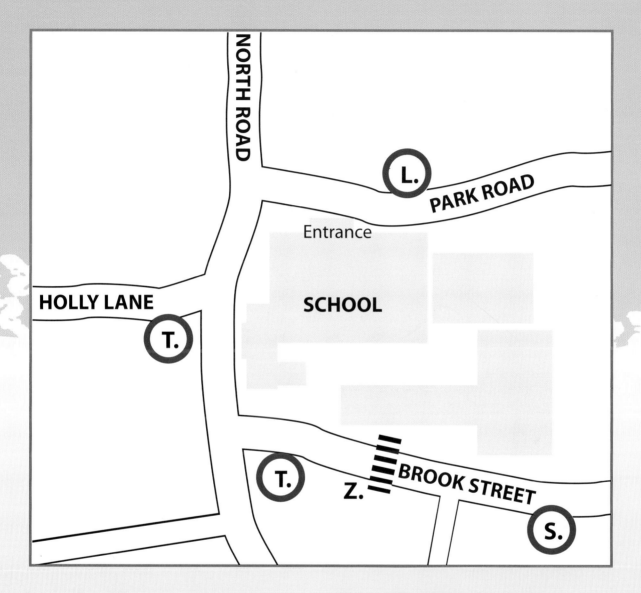

L = Lollipop person   T = Traffic lights
S = Speed sign   Z = Zebra crossing

Which traffic control is nearest to the school entrance? Which one is furthest away?

Stop, look and listen

To cross the road when there are no traffic controls, you have to stop, look and listen!

Wait on the pavement, away from any parked cars.

Look all around for traffic.

Listen for traffic. You can sometimes hear traffic before you see it.

Cross when there is a safe gap in the traffic.

Why should you keep looking and listening while you cross?

Parking problems

Kareem and his class count the cars parked outside their school. They make a bar chart with their results.

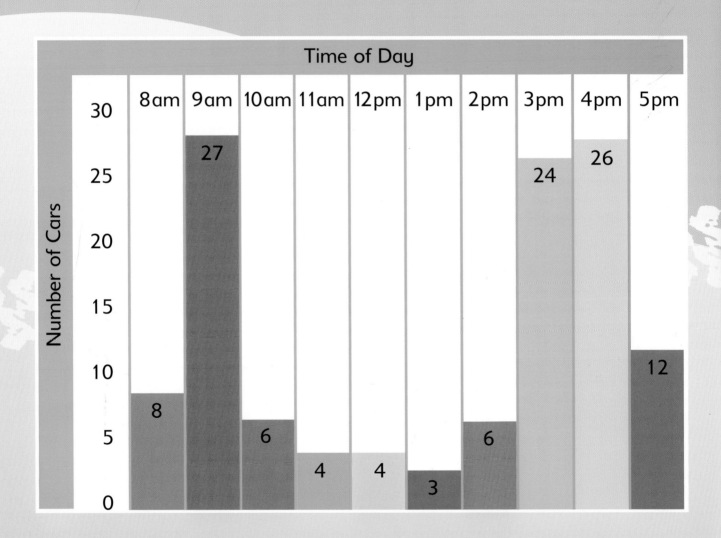

When are there most cars parked outside school? Why do you think that is?

They take photos of the parking problems around their school.

It is not safe to cross the road between the parked cars here because drivers cannot see you.

This car is illegally parked on a double yellow line.

What can they do to solve the parking problems? Turn the page to find out.

Making an area safer

The children in Kareem's class decide to start a 'walking bus' to school with other children and adults. Then there will be fewer cars parked outside.

Why else is it good to walk to school?

Fewer cars also mean less car fumes.
This is good because the fumes
make some of the children cough.

Can you think of any other reasons
why car fumes are harmful?

Old and new

This picture of a road was
taken 50 years ago.

How would you describe this road?
Can you see any traffic controls?

This is the same road today.
What differences can you see?

Which road would you
most like to walk down? Why?

In some countries, traffic means cars, buses and other vehicles with wheels. In other countries, the traffic and roads are different.

Venice is a city in Italy. Here boats are the only traffic because there are canals instead of roads.

Delhi is a city in India. Here people ride bikes, pull rickshaws or use animals to pull carts on the roads.

Bangkok is a city in Thailand. Trains travel across the city and cross over the roads below!

What other kinds of traffic have you seen?

Useful words

Bar chart - a chart that uses bars of different lengths to measure and compare amounts.

Canal - a long and narrow waterway that people build for boats to travel on.

Code - letters or shapes that represent or stand in for real things. Z represents zebra crossing, for example.

Emergency - an accident or serious problem that people need help with straight away.

Local - the area that makes up your neighbourhood.

Passenger - someone who travels in a vehicle that is driven by someone else.

Pedestrian - a person who walks on or by a road.

Rickshaw - a small, two-wheeled cart pulled by a person, sometimes on a bike.

Street plan - a plan that shows all the streets in an area.

Traffic - cars, lorries, buses and other vehicles that travel on a road.

Traffic controls - the use of signs, lights, signals and people to control the flow of traffic.

Walking bus - a group of children who walk to school together with an adult leader at the front and another adult at the back.

Vehicle - a machine with wheels that moves on the road. Cars and motorbikes are vehicles.

Some answers

Here are some answers to the questions we have asked in this book. Don't worry if you had different answers to ours; you may be right, too. Talk through your answers with other people and see if you can explain why they are right.

Page 11: There are a number of other things you can do to be safe on your bike. You should always wear a helmet and learn road safety rules. You could also do a cycling proficiency course.

Page 17: The lollipop person is closest to the school's entrance. The speed sign is furthest away.

Page 19: You should keep looking and listening while you cross a road in case there is any traffic you did not see or traffic that was moving faster than you thought, or in case other traffic suddenly appears.

Page 20: Most cars are parked outside school at 9 o'clock because this is when parents and carers drop their children at school. When the parents and carers leave and go home or go to work, there are hardly any cars parked outside the school.

Page 22: Another reason it is good to walk to school is that walking is good for your health. Exercise keeps you fit and healthy and fresh air helps to wake you up so you can concentrate at school better!

Page 23: Car fumes are harmful to the environment because they contribute to global warming. Global warming is a gradual increase in the Earth's temperature.

Page 24: There is a traffic light to the left of the picture.

Page 25: There are lots more pedestrians, cars and buses. There are also more traffic controls, such as traffic lights and road markings.

Index

cyclists 11
old and new 24–25
parking problems 20–21
pedestrians 10, 15
road safety 10, 11, 13, 14–15
stop, look and listen 18–19

traffic controls 15, 16–17, 18 24, 28
walking bus 22, 28
vehicles 7, 14, 16, 26, 28
emergency 9

About this book

Ways into Geography is designed to encourage children to think about the local and wider world in a geographical way.

This title, **Traffic and Road Safety**, encourages children to think about how we keep safe on the road and how traffic affects our local area. By working through the book, they will be learning the following **geographical skills**:

1. How to ask geographical questions (National Curriculum 1a).
2. To observe and record (National Curriculum 1b).
3. To express their own views about places (National Curriculum 1c).
4. To use geographical vocabulary (National Curriculum 2a).
5. To use maps and plans (National Curriculum 2b, 2c and 2e).

This title also has strong links with PSHE because of the road safety aspects.

Learning content

By using this book, children will also:

1. Learn 'to make observations about where things are located' (National Curriculum 4a).
2. Recognise 'how the environment may be improved or sustained' (National Curriculum 5b). This is touched on in pages 22–23, but you could extend this to look at environmental aspects of pollution, such as its effect on the natural environment.
3. Recognise changes in the environment (National Curriculum 5a) by studying old and new pictures of roads on pages 24–25. To extend work on this topic, you might like to have available an old picture of the school area to compare with the area now.
4. Pages 26–27 will help children to 'identify and describe what places are like' (National Curriculum 3a) and 'recognise how places compare with other places' (National Curriculum 3d). Encourage children to work out why these differences exist.

Previous work

It will help to have done some previous work with the children on using simple maps and to have available a basic street map of the area around the school (from multimap.com, or Google maps, or other sources). You might also want to use a simple mapping package such as Local Studies from Soft Teach, which will enable children to make their own computer maps showing a simplified form of their local area, and some of the traffic controls (pages 16–17).